'Yusuf is a fantastic storyteller. He painted such wonderfully vivid pictures with his words that it felt like I was right there with him as the events unfolded. As a storyteller myself I was inspired by the detail of his observations, and they made me laugh so hard and I felt so connected to them because I could relate to most of his experiences.

Apart from the nostalgia and relatability I found *Living Coloured* to be relevant and necessary in a society that wants to put our identities in a box by telling us what or who we are. This book says proudly that I am enough, my stories do matter, and they are mine to tell.

I'm very jealous I didn't think of this book first.'

– DONOVAN GOLIATH, ARTIST, PRESENTER,
STAND-UP COMIC

Living Coloured

(BECAUSE BLACK & WHITE WERE ALREADY TAKEN)

Yusuf Daniels

JACANA

First published by Jacana Media (Pty) Ltd
First, second and third impression 2019

10 Orange Street
Sunnyside
Auckland Park 2092
South Africa
+2711 628 3200
www.jacana.co.za

ISBN 978-1-4314-2881-6

Cover design by publicide
Editing by Jo-Ann Floris
Proofreading by Joey Kok
Set in Minion 11/13pt
Printed by ABC Press, Cape Town
Job no. 003569

See a complete list of Jacana titles at www.jacana.co.za

786

*This book is dedicated to my mom, Jessie,
and my amazing children, Thameenah, Daanyaal
and Dariya. And to all my Facebook friends who
encouraged and inspired me to keep writing.*

Contents

Acknowledgements

I would firstly like to thank my Creator for giving me this crazy mind, good health and perseverance to write this book. I would also like to acknowledge all the people who played a part in this book becoming a reality.

My mom, Jessie, who always thinks that all my stories are funny. My dad, Isgak, for all that he has done for me. Nau-sheen Wadee for telling me I was destined for bigger things. Sharlene Troskie and Kelly Hendricks for being honest when I sent them my stories to read, and for encouraging me to write this book. To my friend Sean Sullivan in the United Kingdom who keeps telling me 'you're the next Trevor Noah', and also kept on insisting I write this book. To Ismael Jattiem and Nau-sheen for coming up with the 'Living Coloured' portion of my book title.

My Facebook followers who inspired me with all their great comments and some who said they would buy my book if I ever decided to do one. Well, here it is. To my publisher, Nadia Goetham at Jacana Media, who had the faith in my stories and for giving me the chance to publish this book.

A special thanks to Natasha Fakier, who went behind my back and sent three stories to Jacana Media and then the hard yards in helping me shape this book. Last but not least, to my three dragons, Thameenah, Daanyaal and Dariya, who always checked on my progress and shared in the excitement of their dad becoming a published author.

Introduction

I COULD TELL YOU that some amazing event happened that inspired me to write this book, but I would only be lying. I wrote my first story on 29 October 2018. With five needles stuck in my head and another five in my groin, I was flat on my back getting acupuncture treatment at the time. As I lay there looking across the room all I could see and focus on was a big pack of toilet rolls. I thought to myself 'there is no way I'm staring at those toilet rolls for an hour', so I took out my phone and started typing what I was experiencing right at that moment on that bed. I posted it on Facebook and the response was unbelievable.

The true inspiration to write this book is what followed that first post. I wrote another story and another, posted them and people responded with messages of how my writing had made their day. Many loved the humour while others identified with the memories the stories evoked.

Soon I had written 10 stories. A friend told me that

she and her family shared my stories over dinner and they had some great laughs. Feedback like this and the encouragement from my Facebook followers inspired me to write more and also take note of calls for me to write a book.

My good friend Natasha Fakier, who is also my agent now, took it upon herself to submit three stories to two publishing houses and a few newspapers, too, in the hopes that someone would offer to publish my work. Three weeks after writing my first batch of stories, Natasha received e-mails from two publishers, and soon thereafter an offer to publish a book. Having never written a story before, nor a love letter for that matter, I was to be given this great opportunity. Now if that is not inspiring, I don't know what is, right? I knew that the Almighty had new plans for me.

In the following weeks, more and more people started loving my stories and it became an absolute pleasure sharing my childhood memories with everyone. To say that everything happened fast and that it felt very surreal would be an understatement. Like my stories from yesteryear, the story of how I became a published author will certainly be among my favourites.

The stories featured here track my life and, in particular, my childhood while growing up on the Cape Flats. I lived in Bridgetown until I was 10, then in Portlands, Mitchells Plain for about five years and finally in Surrey Estate for a while. No one ever called it by its official name, Portland. It is a collection of my most vivid memories, which carries with it a range of emotions, lovable characters and a glance at a community that found ways of coping with the horrors of apartheid. Sometimes it may seem as if my recollections are stripped of the harrowing oppression, the poor living conditions, the legalised segregation and the systemic racism. But I ask of you, the reader, to see these memories through the eyes of a child who mostly did not know of better at the time. My goal was to tap into the humour of which there was plenty, the love among a community of friends and families, and the resilience that speaks for itself.

Through the process of writing and now publishing this book, I am humbled by what God has given me, and grateful for you and your support. I could never have imagined this would be my life, as I am just a regular Cape Town guy who has grown to love sharing his memories and having you all reminisce with me.

We all have a path that we're following, and my advice to you is not to look too far ahead into the future but rather to live in the moment because new and exciting things will come your way when the time is right. I'm living proof of it. So don't forget that you, the reader, are the inspiration for *Living Coloured*, and for that I am thankful.

Aunty Farieda's birthday party

IN MY FAMILY, I WAS THE ONLY BOY among four sisters. This, on more than a few occasions, meant that I was treated just like one of the girls. Let me explain.

It was Saturday and we are meant to go to Aunty Farieda's 50th birthday party in Snowdrop Square, Bridgetown. By the way, that is where I was born. In a two-bedroom house where Jessie and my dad stayed in the one room, and my sisters, Fadia, Farieda, Gairo and Naas, and I in the other one. Close confines, but we were just fine.

So, the Friday night before, we start preparing for the party. I'm the first one to take a bath. A quarter of the bath is filled with cold water while a kettle of water is on the boil. Jessie then adds the hot water to the bathwater. I'm sitting in the bath and that boiling water is poured into the bath while I'm in it… no man, not over me, on the side. And just you try and complain it's hot, and you'll soema get a waslap through your face. Mom's rules mos.

The Sunlight soap gets rubbed onto the rough wash cloth, and your hair also gets a good scrubbing with the same soap. Welcome to the hood, people. There was no time for fancy shampoo and conditioner. Wow, but my hair used to shine befok in the sun after that wash.

Next step was to towel dry your hair a little; then on goes the swirlkous (not that I needed it). My mother's old nylon pantyhose now transformed into head gear. The upright hairdryer is brought out, and my head gets pushed under its dome. There were no hand-held hairdryers back then.

Fok, it was at least 60 degrees Celsius under that thing, but sit you must. I could hardly breathe as hot air blew down my head and neck. Soon the blisters would start to show on my neck. And just you try and move your body away from that dome; it's game over and my mother would sort me out.

But when I emerged from that dryer and the swirlkous was pulled off my head ... jarre, I became the original 1970s Justin Bieber. My hair was now straight and laid lekka flat against my forehead.

Next it was my sisters' turn. Their hair got the hair rollers and then the swirlkous. Now, you must understand that not all my sisters had 'type 1' hair like me, some of them had 'type 4' or 'stoute hare'; but they all went through the same hair drying/styling process like my hair did. And sometimes, with the rollers intact, their heads would jam under that dome and then my dad had to fetch a shifting spanner to adjust the dome a little. Once everyone's hair has been washed we head for bed with great anticipation for the party the next day.

Saturday morning and we are all up early. I'm in my bottle green suit with moerse bellbottoms. I had swagger from an early age, even if I say so myself. All dressed up, we pile into our VW Beetle and off we go.

Five children on the backseat, we first head to the post office in Cape Town where Mr Van Kalke will be meeting us to take a family photograph. Everybody in Cape Town has a Van Kalke family portrait and we are no different.

Family portrait done and we are on our way again. We arrive at the party and we literally fall out of the car. My dad looks at us one by one and asks, 'Hoekom is julle so blerrie gekrikkel?'

And I'm thinking to myself, maybe because your five children sat on a two-seater back seat, Dad! How could we not get our clothes wrinkled? Of course, I couldn't say this to him. Imagine! We had respect for our parents and, to be honest, we were just downright vrek scared of them so no back-chatting ever. I tell you, today's youngsters would not survive with our parents from yesteryear.

The party was rocking with Peaches and Herb songs klopping on the music centre. A few uncles and aunties were showing off their moves, and there was always that one uncle who had to overdo it. As soon as the music mix made way for a faster Boney M song, enter Uncle Allie onto the dance area. And he was a big show-off. Everybody had to literally take a step back to make the circle bigger and give him space. I'm still not sure what you call those moves, but it was very traumatising to watch as a youngster. You could see he thought he was giving us a great show … breaking it down for us.

We were still watching oepe bek when suddenly his body went into spasm and he looked like he had lockjaw in his back. I kid you not, Uncle Allie lay on the floor with his back completely in his chops. The men had to carry him to one of the bedrooms to rest and sleep off this hectic muscle spasm and pain. Shame, but at the same time, what a relief that we didn't have to watch that display any longer.

Back to the party and we all went on dancing, eating ourselves dik and having a lekka time with all the aunties, uncles and cousins. Anyways, I grew up with four sisters in one room and I think I turned out pretty okay. Ja, okay man, I used to wear their heels sometimes. Oh, and the party was lekka and so was Aunty Farieda on her 50th. Bless her soul.

True story.

Maiden's Cove family picnic

It was Sunday morning in Akasialaan in Bridgetown and the entire Daniels family was on their way to Maiden's Cove Beach. Now take note, this was a big deal because we didn't go to the beach that often. We were vrek excited! Our white VW Beetle, which was just too small to take the entire family and the extras to the beach, was filled up and ready to make the two round trips. Dad Isgak was busy with some chores so he wasn't going to join us.

The extras were the usual – the large pot of breyani, a big Tupperware with the soutvleis sandwiches and gesmoorde egg ones too. Then there was another container with the roast chicken and potatoes, a bowl with salad, the watermelon, a cooler bag filled to the top with Amla drinks and water, the small gas stove (because we must heat up the breyani mos), and three large blankets and some pillows. This is just some of the items we were taking with us. But, yes, we basically packed up half the house.

For those of you who don't know, Maiden's Cove lies between Clifton and Camps Bay beaches. It was the Coloured beach back then. I was about seven years old and didn't even know that the whites-only Clifton Beach existed and was off-limits to the Coloureds. I'm pretty sure just like they didn't allow Coloureds on that beach, they probably wouldn't have allowed large breyani pots there either.

Mom was the driver that day and when she was back from the second trip, we set up our picnic spot and raced to the tidal pool. The youngest of my sisters, Shanaaz, we called her Naas, was always the voo'barige one and soema ran for the pool without any adult supervision. She couldn't swim, and I think on this day she completely forgot this tiny detail herself.

But let me tell you about Naas first. She is two years older than me and back then she was vrek stout. This one did things her way and always landed in trouble. She was the only child I know who got a hiding on her birthday. And because she was deurmekaar, she decided that she was not going to slamse skool – Madressa – on her birthday. So my mom, Jessie, gave her a helse hiding, on her birthday.

On another occasion she decided to skip over the kettle chord while the kettle was boiling. The kettle was on the table, so the chord was hanging between the wall and the table. I have never in my life heard such a loud scream as when that fully boiled kettle ended up on her whole arm. She still looks like a burnt quarter chicken today.

Back to Maiden's Cove. There she flies past everyone along the side of the pool and soema goois a platpens dive into the deep end. Now remember, Naas couldn't a fok swim. I'm watching this move from the sidelines, and I'm thinking, 'haai fok, you're not my brightest sister, hey?' At this point Naas is struggling to stay afloat. All you hear is, blup-blup, blup-blup, and I'm sure by this time she's swallowed about a litre of water. And next thing she started tjanking and swallowing more water, all at the same time. She mos thinks she's kwaai, so let's see who's kwaai now, man-from-Atlantis wannabe.

I don't raise the alarm yet, because I wanted to see how long she could stay under the water. I know, I know ... not very nice of me.

Up she comes and I hear blup-blup, blup-blup again. Plus, that was saltwater and I've heard it's very good for the body. Her head disappears underwater again and I'm thinking: 'Okay, her insides should be lekka clean by now.' So I start shouting at the top of my voice, 'Mammieee, Naas is vesyping', finally alerting her to the possible drowning.

Now my mom was a great swimmer. Next thing, she charges into that pool, five or six strokes later and she soema have Naas by her hair, pulling her out of the water and onto the sand. Now, we both know if this had happened today, the child would have been handled with care. 'Oh, my baby, are you okay?' 'Oh, my baby, did you swallow any water?'

But this is not how Jessie rolled. The water is flowing out of Naas's nose and mouth. And I swear I saw a little guppy jump out of her nose. While all this is happening, Mom is hitting my sister's gat. 'Why did you jump in? You know you can't swim. You're my most disobedient child! Jy moet soema vesyp het, want djy willie hoorie!' Yoh, my mom was cross, hey.

And, of course, I'm just laughing me klaar at Naas. I always enjoyed it when Naas got into trouble, because it took the attention off me, which means I could get away with a lot.

Finally, things settled down and we enjoyed the rest of the day. Naas recovered and we tucked into the lekka breyani and watermelon. I used to eat the watermelon past the white part under the skin.

But I'm telling you this story to remind you that my sisters, and especially Naas, always had my back. Yes, I used to give her grief, but she is my biggest supporter. If anyone messes with her little 40-odd-year-old brother, she would defend me to the bitter end. I can hear her voice: 'Die is nou weer my broer, djy!'

This is what I call family, and we all have that one sibling or cousin who, like Naas, is always entertaining and always lands in deep shit, but will fight for you to the bitter end.

Our beach picnics at Maiden's Cove was a big deal and we have similar great memories of family time spent at Harmony Park, Soetwater and a few other summer spots. Some of you should ask your children where Maiden's Cove is to hear their responses. It's mos just Clifton and Camps Bay these days.

True story.

District Six Kaapse Klopse and the Malay choir

DISTRICT SIX. MY GRANNY'S HOUSE on Plymouth Road. What lekka memories come to mind, nuh!

My granny's name was Ragmat and she didn't take drama, not from anyone! We called her Mamma. A lovely woman, but quite stern when she had to be. She had that little bit of stubble just above her top lip … just so you know who was in charge, lekke astrant mos.

I was clearly one of her favourites. On Eid day my sisters would all get 1 cent and I used to get 2 cents.

My one sister used to complain to our mom, 'Maa' Mammie, hoeko' kry Yusie dan meer as o's en hy issie jongste?' I used to think, ag, Mamma just loves me more. Haaties vir jou, I think, it's just too bad.

Allow me to invite you into Mamma's house. During school holidays we would sleep over at her place for a few days. At bath time we'd fetch that big aluminium bath from beneath the staircase and we'd fill it up with boiled water from the kettle. Out came the Lifebuoy soap to wash our hair and bodies. Watse fancy soaps! A bietjie Dettol also got poured into the bath to get rid of all the germs.

But beware, misbehave in that bath and motjie Ragmat will slaan your gat. I don't even want to mention that wire brush she used to comb our hair with. Let's just say if you were using that brush today on a child's hair, you would be jailed for child abuse.

Mamma didn't have a hairdryer, and you'd get told: 'Go stand on the stoep to dry your hair.' And you'd hope there's a breeze, or you would be parking on that stoep for a while waiting for your hair to dry.

The house also had an outdoor toilet that was always stocked with two-ply newspaper. Yes, you heard me, we used newspaper to wipe, and if you missed any story from that edition, you could probably still find the imprint on my holletjie – my butt.

We mostly stayed with Mamma during December holidays and specifically around New Year's Eve. This was the time when the Klopse and the atchas came out. The atchas refer to the minstrels who wore the weird masks and replicas of devil faces. As children we were vrek scared of them and my granny knew this. They were called Kamalie se Atchas.

She used to look forward to this time.

They would come walking up the road and we would hear that drumming sound that only they made. Fok, my sisters and I would immediately take cover under Mamma's bed. I swear I'd peed my pants a few times under that bed, and Mamma probably wondered why her shoes were so wet. The worst thing was that she and my uncles would guide these crazy people straight to the bedroom and point us out. Have you ever heard a group of children crying and screaming for dear life? That was us – scared, screaming and the adults laughing lekka at us.

One year my dad and my uncle decided they would start their own Klopse troupe. I was about seven years old and about to be part of the minstrel festival!

My mom, Jessie, and Aunty Koelie were seamstresses and made about 1 000 uniforms. They sewed till their doekies were sitting skew on their heads. It took them a few days to complete the costumes, with an hour's sleep here and there.

My uniform was one of the first ones to be sewn. Jarre, I was styling. Our uniform colours were pink, white and blue – all in satin, with an umbrella and a miniature walking stick draped in the same colours. Soon, we were ready for New Year's Eve.

Dancing down the streets of District Six on our way to my aunt's house where she had a table full of treats waiting. My face was fully painted as I hit that stick on the street to the beat of the band music. I don't want to seem like a show-off, hey, but I had some serious dance moves back then. It was like one big carnival right outside my aunty's house, with the whole neighbourhood coming out to watch. Then we were ready to move into the streets and show off to the community.

My uncle, Boeta Manie, used to keep an eye on me during the parade. He was a very big man and had long hair, hence we called him Manie Hare. He used to put me on his shoulders when I got tired, so I had quite a lekka view of what was happening. Remember I was seven years old and after a few hours of jolling I got lekka tired. It was a whole day affair and it all ended at Athlone Stadium or Hartleyvale Stadium, where all the different troupes competed in the various singing categories. That year our troupe took the prize for Best Dressed group. Mom and Aunty Koelie were so proud of their achievement. After the prizegiving we would head to Salt River for yet another table of treats and celebrations at Nanna's house. By 1am we were still at it, and I'm in a semi-coma of tiredness. Poor Boeta Manie had to carry me everywhere.

There were so many traditions that are still going strong till today. My dad and I also sang in a Malay choir, the Starlites. This was a bit more relaxed than the Klopse although we would also sing and dance the night away and end up competing with other choirs at Athlone Stadium. We also used to compete at the Three Arts Theatre back then.

This was a slightly more posh affair because you had to suit and tie yourself. The competition was fierce and we'd pull out all the stops to see who goes home with the most trophies on the night. We sported cream suits, burgundy shirts, and cream and burgundy ties. And remember, these were three-piece suits, which meant we wore cream waistcoats too. The final touch to the outfit was a reddish kwas kofia. Wow, we were styling!

The days in District Six were the good old days. We ran about freely; we played with everyone; we were safe there.

My other grandfather also lived in the area and we would run between his Bloemhoff flat and Mamma's frequently because it was safe to do so. Even the gangsters back then had respect for older people, and if they tried their luck with any of us, my uncles would give them a moerse klap, no change.

Those were the good memories. But the Group Areas Act of 1950 changed everything. In the 1970s, we were forcefully removed from our homes in District Six, and we had to move to unfamiliar spaces and start afresh. The apartheid government took so much from us, but our community's enduring spirit helped us maintain our sanity in the face of much adversity.

Ironically, a good few years back, my parents, my sister

and I were on the front page of *The Argus* as the first Coloured family to move back into District Six. Imagine. First we were not good enough to live there, now we make the paper on our return!

True story.

Don't mess with Ruthie

BACK IN BRIDGETOWN AT 19 AKASIALAAN. A great neighbourhood, lekka people and everybody in the street were tight with each other. I was about nine years old and it was a Sunday afternoon just after lunch. The whole street was busy; parents, children and even the dogs were outside. About 40 of the neighbourhood's people were playing kennetjie outside, a favourite game among the children and adults alike. I was pretty good at it.

Now let me introduce you to Ruth, our neighbour's daughter. A bit on the big side for a 17-year-old and mentally disadvantaged.

Me being the dom nine-year-old at the time used to make fun of Ruth all the time. I know, not one of my proud moments. I would tease her relentlessly, calling her names and making funny faces at her, because I knew that she was not allowed past their front yard gate. This knowledge made me very bold … actually, we can call it what it was. I was sterk gevriet. Untouchable. Or so I thought.

Until that day when everyone in the street was playing kennetjie. I was fielding about ten metres away from Ruthie's front gate, waiting for someone to hit that kennetjie my way. Of course, while I was fielding I was also teasing Ruthie.

Then suddenly the airborne kennetjie was hit in the direction of Ruthie. I ran and leapt right across the pavement, because there is no way that I'm not catching that kennetjie. As I leapt I realised that I'm going to dive straight into Ruthie's gate. Kassam. My full body slammed straight into the gate and as God is my witness, the gate pops open. I looked up and thought: 'God, I ask for 'maaf for making fun of Ruthie all these years. Please protect me.'

Ai, but it was too late. Ruthie was out of their yard like a gazelle and next thing her hands were around my neck and choking the shit out of me. Out of the corner of my eye I saw the other neighbour Mrs Cox touch the rosary she wore around her neck, while saying: 'Oooh jinne, die kind gaan dood vandag.' Yes, I could lipread a little mos, even back then.

First thing out of my mouth was: 'Our Father, who art in Heaven, hello be Thy name.' This was the first time in my life that I forgot I was a Muslim. I soema' forgot my Kalima. And all I heard out of Ruthie's mouth was: 'Wie is nou mal? Wie is nou mal?' And I was shouting back at her: 'Ek is mal, Ruthie. Ek is mal!'

But no, Ruthie was not having any of my pleas. She had made up her mind and it was clear that today I am going to die.

Mr Mentor, Mr Wasserfal, Mrs Cox and half the neighbourhood tried to get Ruthie off of me. I was starting to turn blue in the face when they finally pried her hands from around my scrawny neck.

Immediately I was known as the one who was taught

a lesson by Ruthie. My cool status was gone. Over. And I was now Ruthie's bitch. This was clear because after that incident she would have a satisfied grin on her face whenever I walked past her.

But let me take the positive from this moer session. Playing in the street with all the children from the neighbourhood would become a memory I'd always cherish. The atmosphere was amazing.

We always had respect for our elders. One step out of line and we would be taught a lesson. Unless you want to be embarrassed with a lekka sloffie hiding in front of your whole neighbourhood. No thank you. Not like I haven't had my fair share of embarrassing moments. Just ask Ruthie.

Moral of the story. Payback is a bitch. May God bless Ruthie's soul and all those lovely neighbours we had.

True story.

Childhood games

WHAT GAMES DO YOU REMEMBER playing as a kid? I'm not talking of PlayStation. I'm talking about games we played mostly outside. Here's some of the games that kept us entertained as kids.

Bok bok, hoeveel op die rug

One person standing upright against the wall and the rest all bending down holding on to each other's bums allowing the other team to jump on their backs. The first jumper needs to get as close to the upright person, leaving space for his fellow jumpers. And if you fall off, it's the other team's turn to jump. Or the team bending has a number between one and ten, and if you guess it right the teams swop. Now I always jumped first because I was a moerse kwaai jumper, hey. Soema right to the front. And if it was a girl standing upright in front, haaties, I soema grab onto your boobs to hold on for dear life. I liked that part of the game.

Kennetjie

You cut about 15 cm off a broomstick.

Then you carve the ends so that they are slimmer than the middle part. You rest the kennetjie on two bricks, and with a longer stick, flip that kennetjie as far as possible. Now you guys know from my other story with Ruthie that I was a kennetjie king. We were sometimes 20–30 people playing kennetjie in the street. You flip that kennetjie with the bigger stick and you moerrr it down the road. If they catch you, you're out. We used to hit that kennetjie from the one corner of the road to the other.

Skalòllie (knicks)

It also has a few other names, but Skalòllie is the one we grew up with. Two teams and a ball. Someone rolls the ball to someone from the opposing team and calls out their name. That person kicks the life out of that ball and tries to make it to the other side. The fielding team tries to throw you out or catch the ball.

Now I don't know about you guys, but we had this one kid who would always bring his ball. Now he had a kwaai ball, so we liked playing with his – a leather Mitre ball that kicked lekka. Now if he doesn't get his way in the game or if he gets thrown out, he picks up his ball and says, 'ek willie meer speel nie.'

This was James (Jamesie). He used to work on my last nerve when he did this. If Jamesie left with his ball, it meant we had to play with my nwatta (crap) plastic ball. You kick my ball straight and it ends up 4 m to the right. Jissis, used to toon that ball, hey.

Seeto seet (hide and seek)

One person stands against a pole or a wall, closes their

eyes and counts to 50 or soema 100 while the rest of us has to hide. If that person finds you, they run back to the pole or wall and block you. If you get there before them, you free yourself and you get to hide again.

Now I used to like hiding with Claudine. Let's just say she knew all the kwaai spots. I soema play my own game there in the bush with Claudine. So the person who's counting can either count or shout out stuff like the following to see if we were ready. Anyway, this is how we pronounced it. And please don't judge: SEETO SEET, then we would shout, NAUGHT YET. SEETO SEET, NAUGHT YET. I think it was meant to be, Hide and seek, not yet. But let's not get too technical. Some other ones were, 'Ek koep 'n boksie metjies', then we would shout, 'Die winkel is toe'. That meant you're not ready for them to come looking for you yet. As soon as you shout, 'die winkel is oep', then they can come and search for you. Another one was, 'bruin papier, hol afvee'. Don't even ask.

Handies (Five stones)

Now this was more of a girls' game but we also played sometimes, and I was nogals not too bad at it. You toss five stones in the air and try to catch them on the back of your hand and flip it back and catch it again. My sister was good at this hey, only because she could probably fit ten stones on the back of her hand. She had big hands and if she klapped you, you stayed klapped.

Peaguts

One person standing in the middle of the street and the rest of us must try and run past them without being caught. This game got more difficult as it went on. As they catch people trying to cross to the other side, you now have to get past more people. I was quick and had one hell of a sidestep someone while running. I was in most cases the last person standing. Almost broke my ankle a few times trying to sidestep. Have you ever tried to sidestep someone while running bare feet at full pace on a tar road? I was that guy.

Many times some of the parents would play with us then it soema became a full-on street game, while other parents were just watching, throwing their comments around. Sometimes when I would get out in a game early or get caught out early, I would cry. Ja man, I was a bietjie of a tjankgat.

Then my mom would stand at the gate and shout at me to go inside the house and cry it off. Five minutes later I would come back out and rejoin the game, then everyone would clap hands cause I'm now all tjanked out.

Here are some of the other games that we played that come to mind: a goose, king king, aan-aan, dodgeball, drie stokkies, drie blikkies, and there was also one of my favourite games – road tennis.

Wimbledon courts were drawn in the streets using a piece of brick and tennis bats we made ourselves from just about any piece of wood we could find. I was Björn Borg of course because I had long hair and I used my mommie's swirlkous to put around my head as a sweatband. I was the Akasialaan champion for many years.

It was not just two or three kids playing in the street – we were a community playing together, including parents. We were not glued to TV sets or computer games, we were running around like crazy kids, hitting, jumping, showing off our skills and just having loads of fun.

I can still see myself running in the streets, falling and scraping my knees on those tarred roads or gravel patches. I would cry (tjankie Charlie) for a short while, my mom would put some Dettol on, which burnt the hell out of it, patch it up, and back outside I would go.

By the end of that day we needed a serious bath as we were beyond dirty and tomorrow we would just start all over again. Growing up back in the day was nothing short of amazing.

Maybe sometime you should play one of these games with your kids. They might just enjoy it.

True story.

The Ertjie Dam

THE ERTJIE DAM (PRONOUNCED AIRCHEE DUM) was our playground growing up in Bridgetown.

Let me explain to you where the Ertjie Dam is and how I think it got its name. Those of you who are familiar with the Nantes, a park in Bridgetown, will know exactly where it is. The Ertjie Dam river runs right through the middle of the Nantes and right through Bridgetown. There were pea-like plants that grew all around the river and that's where it got its name from. Now this river was where we would hang out most of our afternoons. On either side of the river you would have a stretch of bush and some trees. A kid's dream when he thinks he's a hunter or in a Tarzan movie.

One day myself, Faizel, Dienie and Nazeem took our ketties – catapults – and a few stones in the pocket, and off we headed to Ertjie Dam. It was adventure time. Dienie spotted a few birds landing not too far from us and we are now all lying flat in the middle of the bush, trying not to scare the birds.

We each loaded our ketties with a stone, ready to shoot down one of these birds as they take off into the sky. Now Dienie was the kettie king. He never missed. So we are all very quiet and watching about 30 birds just feeding and roaming around on a small open patch of grass.

Dienie threw a stone in their direction, and as they took off into the sky, our ketties were out in a flash and all four of us shot in the direction of the birds. I kid you not, Dienie hits one of those birds and all you see is this bird balanging out of the sky. Free fall. Damn, Dienie was a great shot, hey. Off we go to go and claim our prize and now at least lunch is covered.

We made a small fire, Dienie plucked the bird, put it on the fire and we soema had our own little braai going. We had a tin of tomato puree and a very small pot to heat it in. Lekka bird and gesmoorde tamatie on the menu. It tasted just like chicken and hit the spot. Then we were off on the next adventure.

Shoes off and walking downstream towards the N2. The sand was so soft in that river and the water so clear you could see right to the bottom. We even had some spots that were as high as our waists, and made them our swimming areas. There were no parents around, so swimming on a full stomach was not a problem. We didn't have to wait for 30 minutes before swimming. That water was just amazing. We did not have a care in the world, and we had fun. There were also lots of caves on the banks of the Ertjie Dam where we would just hang out and make up stories and pretend we're in some sort of adventure movie.

So we played lekka in the river, and out of nowhere, about six boys rock up and start going at us. Now these boys were from the other side of the river, Silvertown or Kewtown.

Little did they know that we had Dienie, the kettie

king, Faizel who could hit you with that kettie with his eyes closed, Nazeem who could shoot as far as the eye could see, and me. Well, I was just there for moral support.

The talks were now getting heated, everybody's ketties were now out of their pockets and this was only going one way. A little bit of trash talk and some 'jou ma is so vet' jokes and you could feel that things were about to get rough.

Dienie was first to strike. Raised his kettie and shot one of those kids full on into the chest. All you hear is, 'jou ma se ... jy gaan nou sien.'

Jarre, the ding was about to ruk. So we were on the one side and they on the other. We took cover behind some trees and unlucky for them they only had bush.

The stones are now flying back and forth. Now I don't know if you have ever been shot by a kettie, but when that stone hits you, it leaves a little damage and it's vrek sore. Besides the stones now flying across that river, there were some serious swear words also making their way back and forth.

Let's just say Faizel had a vuil bek and was very creative when it came to swearing. So these kids were getting even more pissed off because Faizel was winning that battle. I still don't know how he managed to mention five swear words in one sentence. After Faizel finished swearing at you, you needed a shower.

I remember Faizel swearing at this one kid the one day and this kid was so rattled that his response was, 'ja, but my ma is by die werk.' You just don't get into a swearing battle with Faizel. You're making yourself late. That boy will mention parts of the body that you have never heard of.

But now when your stones run out, you are basically down and you have to run back home for dear life.

I think I was on my last three stones and I spotted this

one laaitie standing up from the bush shouting loudly, 'mis perrepis, mis perrepis'. So to say we can't hit him with our ketties. I loaded my kettie with a lekka fat stone, pulled that tubing back as far as I could for extra velocity and boom, I let go.

I hit that poor laaitie full on the forehead. Bam!

Where does he come off making gat of us like that? All you heard was one big scream of pain and daar tjank 'mis perrepis' nou lekka. I swear from the other side of that river I could see that knop grow on his forehead. He looked like a unicorn within seconds. We were now all laughing so loud and rolling on the ground, while they were swearing at us, promising that they will get revenge.

Ai ja, next time, players. Go back to kettie training, 'cause you were all useless. The blood is flowing from that kid's head and the battle is over. Bridgetown 1, Kewtown 0. Please come again, and don't forget to bring your A-game.

Off they went and we went on about our business as usual. Waiting for the next kettie gang to do battle with.

We were having so much of fun. Our parents knew if we were not in the street, we were at the Ertjie Dam. Those were days and memories that will remain with me forever. We created our own games back in those days and it was safe to roam around places like the Ertjie Dam. One feels kinda bad that the kids today are missing out on adventures like that, but what can they do – it's not even safe to walk around alone in their area. Times sure have changed and the world has become a not so safe place for kids any longer. I wish our kids could experience a 10th of the things we did outside the home.

That being said, I was just happy I got my first kettie victim and I was now the talk of Bridgetown among the chommies. Like, 'don't mess with Yusie hey, he soema shoot you with his kettie against your voorkop'.

Jarre, I felt kwaai. Oh and just by the way, I was actually aiming for his mid-section. I don't know how that stone hit his head. But don't tell anyone.

True story.

Yusie the hustler

Now I was always going to be working for myself or have some sort of business, or sell stuff to someone. Let me explain why I say this. It started out in Bridgetown when I was really young.

The first thing I ever sold was a wetsuit with goggles, flippers and a snorkel my dad brought home from work one day. I sold that wetsuit for R2 that day to a neighbour. I remember he gave me four 50 cent coins and I was the richest person alive. Bill Gates, much later for you.

My dad almost killed me for selling it so cheap, but it was a R2 I didn't have.

Then it was fruit. I used to ask Aunty Milly up the road if I could climb in her berry tree and pick some of the best berries you've ever tasted. I sat in that tree for hours and my clothes were stained all over. Even fell out of that tree a few times, dusted myself off and back to berry picking. I would put the berries in little packets I made from newspaper and sold it to the kids on the street.

Ice blocks was my next venture. I made the best Kool-Aid ice blocks, and for the ones who couldn't afford it, I would take some of my mom's milk from the fridge and soema sell milk ice blocks.

Then I sold toffee apples, which came either with the green syrup or the red syrup. That was a hot seller. Jarre, don't let that syrup get hard – then you gonna struggle to bite through it.

Back to fruit. This time it was lukwats (small yellow fruit that looked like a plum).

Ooh ooh, I almost forgot. I also sold tameletjies, hard-boiled sweets that could break your teeth when you bite into them. Now who of you remember those? So I was selling just about anything to anyone since a very young age. I never asked my parents for money. I had my own money, 'cause I was a hustler.

But this story is around when I was 12 years old and let me tell you something – I was the king of marbles/gatties. I was so good that I had four 5-litre drums filled to the top with all the neighbourhood kids' marbles that I won. Of course then I became a marble salesman.

So this one day myself, Shaheed and Reggie were busy on the field next to Shaheed's house with our usual marble games. We see four kids about our age approaching and thought nothing of it. I remember one of the boys' name was Dino. So Dino and his clan decide they wanna take us on in marbles.

Now Dino of course didn't know that we practically should have gotten our SA colours for marbles if it had to be a sport. These guys brought about 100 marbles each.

All I'm thinking is, 'Dino, vandag kry jy a lesson in marbles'. Dino was a bit of a brekgat. They were from Westridge and we were from Portlands. Westridge people were mos a bietjie sturvie, nose in the air. Right, game on. They unpack all their marbles on the floor and my face just automatically lit up. There were tamaties (red ones), pollies (white ones with different colours), sodas (clear ones), gongs (big ones), ynnies (heavy ones) and more. It was like one huge marble party. I called it easy money. Dino is gaaning aan about how he is the best marble player in Mitchell's Plain and that he has a 5-litre drum of marbles at home.

Blah blah blah. Today I will officially make you my marble bitch, Dino. But I stayed quiet and focused.

That day we played lyntjie, gatjie and poetjie. Go Google it. Now I could hit a small marble from up to 4 metres away. I was that good. As Dino's pockets were getting lighter, mine were just filling up.

Everybody, including some of the neighbours' kids, were now watching me taking over Dino's marble life. I was ruthless when it came to marbles, hey. I am cleaning out this boy and I could see he's getting very upset now. I was already storing some of my winnings in Reggie and Shaheed's pockets. Shaheed even had to get an extra bag to fill up.

And just like that Dino got aggressive. 'Jy, I want all my marbles back'. Those were his words.

Now you don't come into my neighbourhood, be brekerag, lose all your marbles and then demand all your marbles back. So now I have about 10 kids from my area and a few chommies that have my back here. Up against those four boys. You do the math. Now I'm so not parting with my marbles that I won fair and square. And I told Dino to go kruip in his gat and go back to Westridge in no uncertain terms.

Who's the marble king now? Jy maak jou laat, Dino. Dino and co. left with their tails between their legs and I had a new batch of marbles to sell. Back to business as usual. Yusie the hustler. Hahahaaa.

Those days will always stay with me and it's so sad that

our kids will probably not get to experience such things.

And me? I made my own money and sometimes even made loans to my big sisters.

True story.

Heyday treats

LET ME INTRODUCE YOU TO THE things we looked forward to as kids back then that made our neighbourhoods special.

The milk truck

My mom used to leave coupons on the empty glass bottles on our doorstep every morning and the milkman would arrive with his truck, pick up the bottles and coupons and leave us fresh milk, orange juice and guava juice.

This was the best orange and guava juice you have ever tasted. When there was no one around I used to sneak to the fridge and take a few sips, soema from the bottle. I used to mix the two and soema make my own fruit cocktail. Watse Woollies se fruit cocktail! And nobody would steal those bottles off our stoep.

Mr Witton's mobile tuckshop

Then there was Mr Witton and his blue panel van, converted into a mobile tuckshop. He used to come around our neighbourhood every Friday to sell us all kinds of sweets, chips, chocolates and cooldrinks. As soon as we spotted that van in the area, we used to sprint home to tell our moms. As we were running we would scream loudly, 'Mr Witton, Mr Witton'. That was to alert all the neighbours also.

That van was swarmed by kids and moms and Mr Witton's boot would be open in front of our house for at least an hour. All you see are moms taking money out of their bras, at the time the preferred place to stash cash. I don't know what was up with that, but didn't really care 'cause I just wanted my snacks.

Boeta Leiman's fruit and veg truck

Then there was Boeta Leiman, who came around twice a week with his fruit and veg truck, which saved our moms from having to go to the shops. We used to jump on the back of Boeta Leiman's truck as he left and hang on for dear life. I actually mistimed my jump one day on that truck and soema lekka fell me in my glory. It wasn't sore, nuh.

Kyk hoe lekka lieg ek nou.

The uncle with the Bashews truck

Then there was the Bashews truck that dropped off a crate of cooldrink by us every Friday. You would pay him monthly and that crate would be delivered to your doorstep. My favourite flavour was Cocopina. The yellow one. I was so into that drink, I would sometimes have conversations with that bottle while drinking it. Lovingly looking at it between sips I would tell it 'yoh, maar jy's lekka'.

The curly cone truck

Now this was my all-time favourite. My next door neighbour and best friend back then was Dougie (Douglas). We would be playing at the Ertjie Dam, which was about 200 m from our house in Bridgetown.

As soon as we heard that curly cone truck's music playing loudly and spotted that red and white truck, all hell broke loose. We would drop everything, and it was a sprinting race home to tell Mom the curly cone truck is here. Have you ever seen two dirty kids sprinting down a road barefoot on gravel while laughing all the way home? This is how happy we were when we saw that ice-cream truck.

By the time we got to it, there would already be about 20 kids and parents waiting to be served. But that was okay; we had patience and I needed time to think whether I wanted mine with a flake or not.

Now you knew when your mom was a bit tight on the money side, 'cause then you had to order your curly cone with no flake. Some of the ombeskofte kids would soema start shouting 'Waa' gottala, jou ma hettie geld 'ie'. And laugh their asses off.

I remember this one kid Markie, who always had a Flake, and Dougie and I just stared at him while he was making fun of us with no Flakes. One day we were standing there with our Flakeless curly cones and Markie was now singing a song about our mothers who don't have money, and as he collected his cone with the Flake he stared at us with this brekgat look and superior smile.

Next thing, suwallaai kassam, I swear, Markie's whole cone with Flake and all falls out of his hand onto the floor.

The whole neighbourhood is witnessing this and you just hear 'hooooo!' Everybody is in shock, but not Dougie and I.

We burst out laughing and sang at the top of our voices 'my ma hettie geld 'ie en jy hettie 'n cone 'ie'.

Dougie and I never enjoyed our cones as much as that day with Markie staring at that cone and Flake on the dirty gravel. And just like that he picks up that gravelled cone and takes a big lick. He was lekka mossag.

These were some of the highlights for us as kids, and we appreciated every minute of it. And if one of the kids didn't have a curly cone, my mom or one of the neighbours would buy them one. Every kid would get a cone. Our neighbours had each other's backs. I guess we now have to create our own moments with our children. For the price today for one Häagen-Dazs, you could have bought a curly cone for every kid on the street. With a Flake nogals.

True story.

Dangerous daltjies

IT WAS RAMADAAN, THE MONTH of fasting for Muslims, and this one played out in Mitchell's Plain. Now let me just give you a brief description of what goes down in our house and every other Muslim house 20 minutes before it is time to break our fast.

My mom, Jessie, is busy in the kitchen trying to finish the pumpkin fritters that now have to be delivered to just about all our neighbours, as it is custom in our religion to share with others. And guess who must do the deliveries? I soema have three plates at a time and off I go. First stop was Aunty Julie. 'Salaam Aunty Julie, hoe faaa,' I would greet and ask after her well-being.

'Algamdoerilaah my boy, your plate is on the table,' she would respond.

'Kassie Aunty Julie and salaam," I would thank and greet her. She soema gives me a plate of treats that I now have to take back home. Her laaities were kak lazy.

And don't forget Mrs Adams next door also got her

plate, and if it took too long to be delivered, one of her kids, Jackie, Ann or Dennis would be sent over to collect.

Next stop was Ighsaan, and then one more stop, before I start again. Now this story is all about the next stop. Aunty Liema.

Now Aunty Liema had a very oulike daughter, Rashieda. She had long black hair, a figure like a trigger and she was a little older than me. Let's just say Rashieda was more interested in me than Mom's fritters. Whenever I dropped off treats at Aunty Liema, Rashieda would open the door, druk me vas between the curtains, and soema give me a lekka kiss. Aunty Liema was in the kitchen at the time, so she couldn't come to my rescue. Not like I was minding though. Whatever happened between Rashieda and I was all self-defence, and I'm gonna leave that right there. This story however is not about Rashieda.

Aunty Liema also had son called Hiema. This story is about him. We called him Hiematjie. Nice boy, well-mannered, but Hiematjie had one problem. His nose was always running. To such a point where the snot used to rest on his top lip, sometimes for minutes. Now I don't know if he knew that the snot sat there for that long, or if he just used that top lip as a storage unit. Now sometimes that snot soema went past that lip, en as jy weer kyk, snot gone. Hiematjie was a snot magician, it seems.

So one day as I'm standing in Aunty Liema's kitchen waiting for her to give us our boeka treats – to break the fast, in comes Hiematjie with the plates he is delivering to the neighbours. Aunty Liema made daltjies (chilli bites) on this night and it was all packed on her kitchen table. But Hiematjie's hele gevriet is full of snot. I think he had a cold that day 'cause that snot was all colours and lekka thick. In some parts it was drying up already.

And then this happened.

Aunty Liema took that red and white check afdroe lap,

grabs Hiematjie by the neck and swiped that lap across his face. She wiped all that snot with two big swipes clean off his face. I'm thinking 'jarre, Aunty Liema has skills'.

But that's not the worst. She takes that same cloth and she wipes all around those daltjies on the table. And all I'm thinking, 'fok, that is just downright mossag'. I'm so not having daltjies tonight. I was upset hey, 'cause I smaakd a few daltjies this night. All that goes through my mind is 'don't forget to tell Mom, don't forget to tell Mom'. So I get home and first thing I do is tell Mom. Now Aunty Jessie was very hygienic and very prim and proper. She was never gonna touch those snot daltjies. We soema sent that same plate of Aunty Liema further down the road to Aunty Gairo them, 'cause they mos didn't know that it wasn't my mother who made it. Shame for Aunty Gairo, but we couldn't waste it.

Almost time to break our fast now and I'm standing on the stoep waiting for the Maghrieb Athaan, the call to prayer. It was like the Athaan couldn't come soon enough. I hear it and I speed off to that table where my six different savouries were sitting on my plate. As kids you couldn't wait to eat. That plate was finished in under two minutes.

This is just some of the memories of Ramadaan I've shared with you guys. I can go on and on. I'm also sure most of you had a Hiematjie-snot-nose as a friend or in the neighbourhood.

Today we only see in certain areas people sharing and kids delivering boeka plates. How times have changed and how kids are missing out, being grabbed by a Rashieda and having three different kinds of daltjies from three different aunties, affording you the opportunity to decide which is your favourite.

True story.

My first 10-km road race

WHEN I WAS 12 YEARS OLD I found a new passion: I don't know where it came from, but yoh, I just wanted to run. I was like Mitchell's Plain's junior Forrest Gump.

Now we stayed in Portlands and my eldest sister stayed in Lentegeur, and those who know Mitchell's Plain will know that you have to cross a bridge past Portland High to get to Lentegeur. That bridge became my training ground.

Back then we only had landlines, so I would call my sis and tell her when I'm leaving my house and she then would time my run to her place. I was even looking for excuses to run to her, sometimes even twice a day. I became like my mom's courier service to my sister's house.

If I look at it now, it was 2 km to her and 2 km back to my house. So that's 4 km a day, every day. And like I said, sometimes twice a day. At the time I was running about four minutes a kilometre. I kid you not. It was like a semi sprint over that bridge. I ran across that bridge like I stole something. Blerrie vinnag. I ran those sanshoes – my trusted tekkies – in their glory.

After about three months of non-stop running, I was reading the local newspaper, the *Plainsman*, and stumbled across a local 10-km race happening in Woodlands. I told my mom I would love to participate in this race. Mom agreed and had the R2 ready for the entry fee.

I was soooo excited as this would be my first long-distance race. And nogals a 10-km race, which I'd never done before. The race started at Woodlands garage and finished there as well. Saturday morning arrived and Mom and I overslept – we woke up at 7:30am and the race start was 8am. I have never put on my red jogger and white sanshoes so fast. I don't even remember if I brushed my teeth and in a flash Mom Jessie and I was off by foot to Woodlands garage. This meant we had to run to the race and we still had to enter.

We got there about two minutes before the race was due to start and they accepted my entry as Jessie paid the R2. I hardly recovered from that run and the gun went off for the race to start. I was in the under-13 category and there were about 100 kids competing. I started right at the back and off we went.

Within the first kilometre I found myself in front of the pack. I ran past all those kids with no effort. I promise you, I wasn't trying to show off. It was just what I knew – to run, and run fast. I was now running behind the race car. At 4 km in I turn around to see who's behind me and I swear to you, there was no one in sight. I thought maybe these other kids stopped for a lunch break or maybe I took the wrong route. I wasn't very 'running clever' so I had no plan, no race time in mind or wasn't pacing myself. I was having so much fun I was actually trying to catch the race car. I was flying and didn't even realise it. I was now running on my own for most of the race.

All I was thinking was how I was going to spend that R30 prize money. Now R30 for a 12-year-old kid back then was like R1 000 for a kid of today. I was thinking it's time I get myself another jogger besides the red one and maybe a new pair of sanshoes as the pair I was wearing was near to its end from all the mileage I did to my sister's house and back. I was gonna give Mom R5 for her effort to get me to the race. Shaheed and Reggie were gonna get a Jelly Billy sucker each plus a packet of Flings. I know, I'm a great friend, hey! That was big money and it was all mine.

It was just me and the car and I was almost playing a game trying to go past this car. I was having so much fun, man. The driver must have thought I was crazy. Think what you like but this race was mine. I didn't know what the time was and it was not important either. What was important was that Jessie saw me crossing that line first. Whenever my mom was at one of my sporting events, I would excel. I guess she brought the best out in me.

Let me explain to you what I looked like that day. I had a body like Zola Budd and had long hair till in my neck. My mom told me after the race what the announcer had said as the first runner took the final turn to the finish line, which was about 300 m out. These were his words: 'Ladies and gentleman, the first runner is approaching and it looks like we have a young girl in red shorts coming in all on her own.'

My mom said that she was so disappointed because she just couldn't believe it wasn't me. As I came closer she realised it was me after all. She said it was one of her proudest memories of me in a sporting event. She soema cried. I wasn't even tired and as I crossed that finishing line the time said 39 minutes. Yip, I did a 10-km race in 39 minutes at 12 years old. It was crazy.

Today I'm proud of myself if I do a 10-km race in under 50 minutes.

We collected our prize money, I got a medal and was congratulated by many. Some of those kids came in like 30 minutes after me. Maybe they need to run to their sister's and back. Y'all need to do some training to keep up with this Zola Budd.

The walk back home was nothing short of amazing as I had my medal around my neck and my R30 in Jessie's purse. She says I spoke non-stop about the race. I think she's exaggerating.

It's amazing though how special it makes you feel if your parents are around supporting you in whatever you do. I will never forget my mom's face as I crossed that winning line.

Years later I watched my daughter in grade 7 at Rustenburg Junior School at a netball game, and I sat right by the poles where she was shooting. This child broke a new junior school record as she recorded 23 goals on that day. Every time she shot a goal she would stare at me with a smile and a wink. We don't realise how important it is that we support our kids, even if they don't win. I remember when my son scored his first goal for his soccer club, Rygersdal. OMG, it was one of my proudest moments. I actually had to move off to the side away from the crowd as I was shedding a little tear of joy. No man, there must have been a biegie in my eye.

Just to be there means the world to them. I am that netball dad, cricket dad, boxing dad, running dad, soccer dad, rugby dad and sometimes a very moeg dad. But it's all worth it when I see their faces when they see me there.

True story.

Labarang vriete and Christmas pudding

Now I DON'T KNOW ABOUT YOU, but as a 12-year-old kid, Labarang – or Eid, the big feast after a month of fasting – was a big deal. This one played out in Portlands, Mitchell's Plain.

Three weeks prior already my mom and I went to Skipper Bar in the town centre to order my Tycoon suit. With that I had my white Skidgrids and a white Stetson belt. New trunkie from Ackermans and my diamond pattern socks were sorted. To top it off, I had a new London Fog jacket. I was ready for Labarang like Labarang wasn't ready for me.

Now on Labarang myself and Shaheed couldn't just leave Reggie at home just because he was not Muslim, so Reggie soema put one of his lekka Sunday church outfits on and just for today he was Rashaad. Mosque done, and myself and Shaheed were on our way to collect Rashaad to walk the neighbourhood.

Now we knew which house was a Muslim house because of that Moon sticker with the toellies (Arabic writing) on it, displayed on the window. This was the highlight of Labarang. Every house you greet, the aunty gives you money and you can eat some of the treats that's spread out on the table. It's chocolates, cakes, Quality Street sweets, samoosas, pies, daltjies and so much more. It was a vriet fest, I tell you. Our right pockets were filled with coins and our left pockets were filled with sweets. But now Shaheed and I knew we should pace ourselves and didn't eat at every house. But Reggie/Rashaad mos decides he's soema gonna eat at every house and it's pies and cakes and alles at the same time.

We are now at our 15th house of the morning and our next stop is Aunty Tiema's house. Now she had a kwaai house with a Vibracrete wall and a gate with a bell. That was posh back in the day. They also had a new Ford Cortina XR6 in the driveway.

Boeta Achmat, Aunty Tiema's husband, had a very posh job. He was mos a bank teller at NBS bank. Aunty Tiema was known for having the best table spread on Labarang. She was also the only aunty who gave the kids R1 coins she kept in a little bowl. The other aunties all gave 20 cent pieces. Aunty Tiema had a Blaupunkt TV, a double cassette music centre and a Betamax video machine. This aunty was up. A befokte floral lounge suite and wallpaper to match. Aunty Tiema's kids had Jokari roller skates while we all had those strap-over ones.

So by now Reggie is so dik gevriet from all the savouries and chocolates and cooldrinks that he started to go a bit quiet. We greet as we enter Aunty Tiema's house, 'Salaam Aunty Tiema and slamat for Labarang'.

Rashaad knows the drill and he does the same. Now Aunt Tiema had a big punch bowl on the table and yoh, it was the best punch you have ever had. Rashaad is busy eating away again and soema downs a lekka glass of Aunty Tiema's punch while he's at it.

I'm not sure if the punch went down the wrong pipe, but when Shaheed and I turn to him, his whole face changes. I think he swallowed too fast. Aunty Tiema has this confused look on her face and all we hear is 'bhaaaaarf'.

Out of his mouth flew a fountain of pies, samoosas, chocolates, daltjies and a whole lot of other stuff. He throws up the whole day's vriete, and some lands in Aunty Tiema's genuine crystal punch bowl.

All we hear is Aunty Tiema saying: 'Yaaa Allah, maar wat het die kind gevriet?'

'My klong jy kan mossie vir jou so oorvriet nie man.'

That punch bowl now had some extra ingredients. Aunty Tiema was not impressed, hey. Rashaad was so embarrassed, he soema walked out without greeting.

Shaheed and I were so confused and nervous at the same time. I soema took one of the sweets from my pocket and put it on Aunty Tiema's table. Like a peace offering.

When we arrived, that punch bowl was three-quarter full. Now it was filled to the top. Compliments of Rashaad. Oorvriet nog.

We left without me even collecting my R1 from Aunty Tiema. I was naar – upset – with Rashaad. Shaheed and I agreed right there that for Labarang Gadjie (second Eid), Rashaad must be Reggie again and stay with his gat at home.

Besides that incident all went well for the rest of the day. We visited about another 60 houses and after every house we would count our coins that we collected. Yes, it was very time consuming as some of us were a little slow at counting. I won't still mention names, but let's just say this person was not Aunty Tiema's favourite person.

We would still have our Labarang lunch with the

whole family and overeat as always. The next day most of us would be sick. But back in those days our Christian friends and neighbours shared in our Eid celebrations. And the other way around. I would dress up in my Labarang outfit on Christmas and move around with my Christian friends. I was soema Joseph that day. This was a day of family, friends and lekka vriet. And that night when you went to bed, you would count that money you collected for the day one last time. I was now R7 richer. Don't hate please, I walked hard for that money.

True story.

There's a floater in the pool

Now FOR THOSE OF YOU WHO don't know what a drol means, it means poop. Remember this for later in the story.

It's 32 degrees on a lekka hot summer afternoon in Portlands, Mitchell's Plain. School is out and myself, Reggie and Shaheed decide we're going to Westridge pool after school. We spread the word at school and next thing all the standard 5s are soema also going. Including the girls in the English class. Now for some reason those girls were just lekka. I was in an Afrikaans class mos.

School is out, and off we go. Put on my red jogger and sanshoes and soema grabbed the first towel in sight. Off we go down Silversands Road to the public swimming pool. Stop by the shop quick to grab a Jelly Billy and soema put one in the jogger also. Oops, forgot to pay for that one.

In line at the pool now you can already spot who's there. Anthea is there, Aneefa, Chelita, Colleen and Rene also. Now these were the most popular girls and they had the looks to go with it. The English have arrived.

Jarre, today I'm gonna have to show off my diving skills. It is now so hot that Reggie's hair is mincing from the heat and we need to get into that pool. The Jelly Billy sucker in Shaheed's jogger is now also all melted. Now there's jelly on his willy. Hahaha.

In we go and find ourselves a spot near the English girls.

The pool is beyond packed. I'm serious. It was so full you could hardly swim. The girls are checking us out and it's me who dives first. Now I was very kwaai at diving. Jack knife, double flick flack, I could do it all. I slam my feet about six times on that concrete into a beautiful jack knife, and splash, a perfect execution. Come up from under the water and my hair is all to the back like Brooke Shields in *Blue Lagoon*. Reggie and Shaheed give me the thumbs-up to say 'befokte dive'.

The English girls are all smiles and I feel kwaai. I spot Aneefa and the girls going into the pool and we all follow. Now we're all having fun, splashing each other with water, I soema by mistake rub up against Aneefa's boob, because the pool is rather full.

And then this happened.

As we are fooling around in this very full pool, Aneefa and I are getting very familiar with one another. I'm thinking 'today I found myself an English girl'. All I hear is Reggie shouting something like 'hier kom kak'.

My first impression was that something bad is gonna happen, but I see nothing. As I turn to face Aneefa a big, brown drol pops up right between us! I swear it was like a shark was released in that pool.

Aneefa screams 'poop, poop' and all I'm thinking is, 'English girl or not, you're on your own here, girl'. I just wanted to get away from this floater as quickly as possible. Someone decided to make a job right there in the middle of the pool. No man! I have never seen a pool get that empty that quick.

Like the *Man from Atlantis*, I was out that water in a jiff. I was so upset because Aneefa and I were just about to swim through each other's legs under water. I was so mad at that drol, hey. My moment was gone. The pool maintenance man was called in to remove the floating object.

After that incident we lay flat on the paving around the pool area and our bodies dried in no time. When we got up there, we felt like we just came out of a tumble dryer. The rest of the afternoon was spent in and out of that pool, racing one another. We would also throw a coin in the pool and see who would find it first. We would create our own little games, and when we were tired, we would come back out and sometimes just stare at the very lovely lifeguard in her bathing costume, who I would have drowned for all day long. Let's just say she had a little Baywatch babe thing going on.

Well, my first English girl experience was not meant to be, and I'm thinking we shouldn't steal Jelly Billys from the shop again. Karma!

Oh well, that was the best 15 cents I've spent at that public pool. And I got to rub an English girl's boob, although only for two seconds.

True story.

St James Beach eviction

I HAVE FAMILY MEMBERS WHO are fair in complexion, and I have other family members who are darker. You will soon understand why I am explaining this.

It is early on a Sunday morning in Portland, Mitchell's Plain. We are going to St James Beach, next to Muizenberg, for the day.

Aunty Fati and Boeta Manie invited me along for the day. They lived just a little behind us in Michigan Way and had two sons, Shameeg and Fuad. Now if you put myself next to Shameeg and Fuad, you would think we were three white children. We were three really white Coloured kids. Spierwitte kinners.

The cars are packed, and you know mos, it's plenty of food, umbrellas, blankets, breyani pots and alles. We were about five cars and one bakkie packed to capacity. Now I've never been to St James Beach, and Shameeg and I are already talking about how we gonna dive and swim and the games we're going to play. Excited is an understatement. It took us about 20 minutes to get there as Mitchell's Plain wasn't very far from St James Beach.

As we arrive I see a lovely tidal pool and nice picnic spots to set up camp. Carrying all our stuff from the cars onto the beach took us longer than the drive. You know mos we had food to feed a little village. That's just a Coloured thing. Done unpacking and Shameeg and I immediately jumped into our Speedos and jack knife into that tidal pool.

We are now only about five minutes into our pool session when we hear the sirens.

Three police vans pull up and about seven policemen jump out of their vans, heading straight for us. Now this family I'm with were English-speaking people, but obviously could speak Afrikaans as well. Two of the cops come to Shameeg and I, chasing us out of the water and saying 'julle moet onmiddellik uit hierdie water klim'. Now we were 12 and 13 years old respectively at the time, and white people in police uniform back then made us very nervous.

Boeta Manie starts speaking in English to the cops. Now these were all white policemen and all Afrikaans-speaking. And now the main cop wants to show that he can also speak English.

And this comes out of his mouth: 'Yous kallit peoples knows thet this here beach is only for de white peoples. Yous Boesmanne hev your own beaches mos dair by Mnandi Beach side'.

That was their favourite word for us. Boesmanne. 'Dis beech here is only for blankes'.

My first thoughts were 'this tief didn't finish school'. Not with that messed-up range of vocabulary. Definitely not top of his aanpassingsklas, the one for slower learners.

Boeta Manie speaks English to him again, and I think he did it just to see this cop suffer.

He tries to explain we're just here to have fun. Cop wants to hear nothing and says again: 'if you's all one to be gearresteer den pleese ignorer me'. And I'm thinking 'your English teacher will die if he or she must hear you now, Mr Policeman'.

Why didn't he take some of the money he got from his white government and invest it in a lekka English-made-easy-for-idiots cassette (CDs weren't out then)? Or the police force should get an interpreter for all their police units, because this ou just sounded superkak. It was like he spoke a foreign language.

I'm thinking 'Mr Policeman, but myself, Shameeg and Fuad are then whiter than all seven of you cops and some of you look more like Boesmanne than us. Some of them had that Hansie Cronje look. You're not sure if they were white or Coloured. May Hansie rest in peace.

What's up with this white thing? We were confused and all we wanted to do was swim. They threatened us with arrest and we had no choice but to leave. Forcefully removed from St James Beach with two wet children, we had to carry all that stuff back to the cars. We went to Strandfontein Beach and had to go through all the unpacking again. Ended up swimming in the ocean and still had lotsa fun, like only we could.

I could see that Boeta Manie was sad that we had to leave. But this is what we had to live with back in the day as Coloured and Black people. It was dictated to us where we could go to. We had to sit in the back of the bus. We had to sit in the third-class carriage on the train. We couldn't play in certain parks. That moment, that day somehow never left me.

As a kid we just wanted to have fun and didn't really take note of all the political crap. But I could see on all the adults' faces that they were hurt and disgusted.

To all my white friends, I still love y'all and I'm not

gonna blame yous for all your uncles' crap.

Whenever I now go to St James pool I make a wee in that pool and say softly in my head 'Mr Policeman, watch me now. Jou ma se…'

True story.

BMX befok

I WAS AROUND 13 YEARS OLD and just got a new silver and red Mongoose BMX bicycle for my birthday. Now for those of you who don't know, a Mongoose was the top of the range at the time. It was the Lamborghini of BMXs back in those days.

First day and I had to test it out. Reggie and Shaheed are at my house, coming to see my new bike. Now with this bike I could do all kinds of tricks. Pop a wheelie, jump up and down pavements and soema jump over people lying in the road.

Yep, you guessed it right; Reggie was forced to lie in the road so I could test my jumping skills on my new bike. He was the smallest, so he had no choice. The timing of me getting my Mongoose could not have been any better. The following Sunday about 20 of us, aged between 13 and 17, all on bikes, decided we were going to take a ride to Kalk Bay. I was so excited. The morning of the outing I packed my haversack with a clean T-shirt, my jogger to swim in, and my patch and solution, just in case I get a puncture.

Sunday morning around 9am and we're off. Through Rocklands, past Mnandi Beach, then past Strandfontein Pavilion and we are close to Muizenberg. We were riding on Choppers, BMXs, Raleigh racing bikes and one or two guys even had those big black postman bikes. It didn't matter, we were on a mission, and we were having fun. The Mongoose is going like a dream. Picture 20 kids on bikes, all in a row. You know when you see those 20 Harley-Davidson motorcycles coming past you in a row, all proud and noisy on the freeway? Now that's not how we felt. We made more noise than our bikes.

Boom! My friend Mellie has a flat tyre. All bikes pull off on the side of the road, the patch and solution is out in a jiffy. Good timing though, cause I can soema have a little polony sandwich break that Mom Jessie packed for me. This time she nogals put lekka thick tomato sauce on it. Out comes the Kool-Aid that I kept in the freezer overnight, still lekka cold.

Mellie's bike is fixed in no time and off we go again. We arrive in Kalk Bay around 11:30 all sweaty and very hot. We park all our bikes on the sand , ready for a well-deserved swim. Now for those of you who don't know Kalk Bay, this is where the fishing boats dock.

Mellie comes up with this great idea. Who's coming with him to dive down the jetty between the boats and take a 100-m swim across, back to the sand where all our bikes are parked and where we're now actually picnicking?

Not everyone had the pluck to do it. Voor op die wa, that was me – always head in first.

I'm in, and so are four other guys. We run around on the jetty and make sure nobody sees us. The others are now all watching us from the sand side. Mellie makes the first start with a lekka jackknife off the jetty. You didn't need to ask me twice and just like that I dive off that jetty. My red swimming jogger almost ended up by my knees when I landed in that water, and I quickly had to pull it up. All of us are in the water now and swimming across.

This is where things got just a little interesting. Kalk Bay harbour is well known for seals, basking in the sun or just swimming around in the bay. The same bay that we are now swimming in.

All of a sudden we hear Mellie shouting very loudly 'Saak, saak, saak!'

Now remember, Mellie had no front teeth so he missed the H. We look around and all we see is this black fin coming toward us. Ma se... I'm thinking. 'God, let me not be the one swimming at the back of this bunch. Please let Mellie be eaten first because next week I am head waiter at my cousin's wedding, and I cannot miss that.'

That is mos where the shark will start his meal, at the back. Another thing that came to mind when I thought there was a possible shark in this water, was not that I should swim for my life, but that my ma gaan my moer as 'n shark my vandag opvriet. There's no time to think now and we are swimming like Bobby Ewing in *Man from Atlantis*. I'm sure all of us broke some swimming record that day.

As we frantically try to get to dry land, a tugboat pulls in. The captain of this boat decides to shout at us while we are swimming for dear life. Much later for you captain, we're in a race for survival here.

We get to the shore all out of breath and all accounted for. And the other 15 guys are killing themselves with laughter. I am dizzy and can hardly breathe, and these guys are laughing like crazy.

Yip, it was a seal that Mellie mistook for a shark. It was not funny, as I could feel my heart beating outside my chest. We were made fun of for the rest of the day, of course.

Most of these guys belonged to a gang but were all my friends. Bicycle riding gangsters! But we still knew how to have fun and do adventurous things. We had each other and our bikes. Oh, and don't forget the polony sandwiches with the bag of tomato flavoured Crinkle Cut chips and the Kool-Aid to wash it down.

Those chips on that polony sandwich was nothing short of very lekka.

The Mongoose kept up with the pack very nicely that day. I enjoyed my birthday gift to the max. Thanks, Mom and Dad. Our parents always made a plan to keep us happy and I will always be grateful for that.

True story.

Dream big – baseball

Growing up in Mitchell's Plain was rather challenging. When I was around 14 years old I looked up to my older friends who all belonged to a gang called the Hard Livings. When I say gang I mean serious gang with the chappie – tattoo on the body in the form of the gang's name. I did things with them that I'm not very proud of today, but peer pressure was a bitch. Otherwise you were not cool.

Drugs were around and smoking dagga was a big thing. But for some reason I never tried it.

A gang fight back then involved pangas and knives. Some of those friends today are no longer with us and some are barely alive.

Let me tell you what got me out of that whole gangsta buzz.

So myself, Neil, Reggie and Shaheed were walking through a primary school one day, soema throwing stones. Blerrie stout mos. Not too far from us was a guy called Cliffie, who was busy coaching a baseball team. He calls us over and says: 'Julle kan lekka klip gooi nuh, nou kom gooi die blerrie baseball.'

I picked up that baseball and 30 odd years later I'm still throwing it. The first time Jermaine and I played, it was in white shorts and long blue socks. That was at Stephen Reagan sports field in Westridge. We had baseball and softball all at the same fields back then. What an atmosphere.

So the girlies would check us out. Now Woodlands softball juniors had some of the cutest girls, and they would always support us. They were the English girls mos. My team was called Tahiti Braves and we were based in Portland. After the game we would walk the girls home, on a lekka romantic walk. About eight of us or so.

As soon as we dropped them, that romantic walk turned into a moerse sprint. We would be chased by gangstas from the Woodlands area until we reached Portland. And this is why we stayed so thin and fit. We did a lot of running.

Back to the field and we would get a lekka pie and a guava juice and now watch the seniors play their game.

In the second year I made the Mitchell's Plain junior board side. It was nogals advertised in the *Plainsman* newspaper with a pic of me. The whole neighbourhood knew I made that team, and if they didn't, my mom made sure they did. She would go visit everyone and ask them 'het jy gesien, Yusie is in die Mitchell's Plain board side?' She was always proud of me, hey.

Then I played for a club in Salt River called Blackpool. Now this club was known as the Slamse club. Some of the best people I have ever met in my life and still friends of mine today. Yaga, Tapie, Eie, Mac, Niefie, Iqbal, Azeem, Malik, Soelie, Kariem, Faroeki, Dickie and Sevens, to name but a few. And you wanna know why they called it a Slamse club!

And the infamous Coach Toyer. He was like a Hitler with a kofia. Yoh, he worked us hard!

I was so into baseball I couldn't wait for training. I would throw that ball whenever I had a chance. I kept on making the provincial side every year after that. We had interprovincial games and played against teams from Cape District, Western Province, Eastern Province, Transvaal and Natal. Those games had a few thousand people watching.

As my interest in baseball grew, so my interest in gang activities became less. We moved to Surrey Estate when I was 16, and then I played for Cape District. That year, I was the only junior who went to junior and senior trials. I was a first baseman back then. We were fully sponsored and accommodation was paid for.

Today you as a player must fork out a fortune to represent your country. An absolute joke, I think.

I fell completely in love with this sport. Then they discovered I throw the ball pretty hard and I became a pitcher. When I was about 19 all baseball teams started playing under one banner – Western Province. The white and non-white teams all played in one league now. It was even more difficult to make the Western Province team now, but I did. I was now completely away from gangsterism and only focussed on school and baseball.

And girls, of course.

At 24 I was the under-24 South African team captain that went to the All Africa Games in Harare, Zimbabwe. It was my first time travelling. To represent your country was one of the most amazing feelings.

We won all our games and did our country proud. We have the gold medals to show for it. And what made this experience even sweeter was the fact that Jermaine was right there beside me, the same person who started playing baseball with me 10 years ago.

A year later I was called up to the senior South African side that went to the Intercontinental Cup in Havana, Cuba. An experience like no other. Beside the baseball, I think I almost got married three times in that place. The Latino women are mos gorgeous, man.

If there are any Slamse laaities running around in Cuba, it was all in self-defence. Three weeks in Cuba was an absolute dream come true. And when you put on your South African jacket before boarding that plane – man, it made you feel like a dik ding, very important.

I missed out on the Olympic squad to Australia due to what I can just describe as politics and I would even go as far as to say favouritism among certain groups. How could I not make that Olympic team after pitching my club side, Thistles, to league and knockout trophy wins that year?

Ruan also got the same 'hou jou bek, Coloured laaitie-deal' that year as he was one of the better pitchers as well.

One of the top pitchers in that South African squad selected for the Olympics was a player based overseas. He had two brothers who were never part of the SA setup until the Olympics. I am not gonna say which race they were, but their brother was white. These boys were selected ahead of myself and Ruan, and it was never explained to us how this came about. Our dream was stolen from us.

It was very sad for me to see how politics can ruin a young man's dream. I played in the Western Province setup until I was 40 years old and then switched to masters baseball. I am now having the time of my life with all these crazy masters who all played provincial or national baseball at some stage.

Baseball changed my life. I could have chosen the gang route and maybe would not have been able to tell my story. Sport can really be a great medium for kids to channel their energies into and could change one's life. In my case it did.

Politics and unfairness in sport is a long way off from disappearing and I see it today still at all levels. Sad but true.

But thanks to Cliffie for calling me over that day. That right there was a game-changer for me.

So encourage your kids to play sport and support them as much as you can. Whether they achieve or not, they just want to see you as a parent on that sideline cheering them on.

True story.

Fun City ice rink

ONE OF MY FAVOURITE PASTTIMES on the weekend was going to the Fun City ice rink.

I was around 16 or 17 years old when this was our weekend thing. You arrive and there's this moerse long queue. Everybody, and I mean everybody, was there. I never wasted my time in that queue, because my sister's boyfriend was the bouncer. This was the time where I already spotted who I'm going to ask when the DJ announces the time when it's couples skating. There were girls from Bo-Kaap, Salt River, Woodstock, Walmer Estate, Surrey Estate, Mitchell's Plain, Crawford. I can go on and on. So we get inside and you stand in another queue where you hand in your shoes in exchange for a lekka pair of ice skates. Always make sure your blades are sharp, otherwise you fall hard on your bek. And believe me, you don't want to do that in front of all those lovely ladies. And always make sure you have good socks on. Ones with no holes, and a spare pair for after.

Then onto the ice with all my chommies. First we skate anti-clockwise and later the DJ says we have to go the other way. Don't ask me why. Skating graciously – as I could skate pretty decently – I'm just checking out who was in the house.

Now I could show off, hey. Soema into a flip and I'm now skating backwards. I make sure the girls can see my skills, doing some figure eights.

And just then I spotted her. OMG. Juwaiya was her name. Long beautiful black hair hanging down the side of her shoulders. Her beautiful red Alice band and those teardrop earrings. This girl is the reason why I like J.Lo today.

Latino features and a smile that lit up the whole of Fun City. That night she had on her size 28 fitted Emme jeans and a black polo neck with a denim jacket. I was a little shy, so I didn't really have the plak to go over and just introduce myself. I had to be strategic.

I had to now wait for that perfect moment where the DJ announces that it's couples skating. That meant that I had to be close to her, for as soon as the announcement is made I will have to be right in front of her to ask if she wanted to skate with me. Couples skating would mean we get to hold hands and skate for at least 15 minutes.

There was only one problem: Cassiem.

Cassiem was a speed skater and lekka brekerag. I saw him also eyeing Juwaiya the whole night.

I'm thinking 'Yusie, tonight is the night where you make your move'. Cassiem's gonna have to sit this one out. So it's slowly building up towards couples skating and I have Juwaiya in my sight. I spot Cassiem also checking her out and suddenly I don't know what came over me. The DJ announces couples skating and all I'm thinking is 'Cassiem must fall, Cassiem must fall'.

He rushes over to her. Somehow I ended up in his path

and my foot just leaped out, and when I looked again, Cassiem was lying flat on his gevriet on the ice. Hare deurmekaar and sopnat as there was some water in that corner of the rink.

Now Cassiem had stoute hare – 'n bietjie kroes hare – so when he hit that ice, the water that was on the surface wasn't very nice to his hair. There were no GHDs back in the day so Cassiem's hair was very gemince.

Sorry for you, player. He actually ended up right in front of Juwaiya. Accidents do happen and someone had to skate with Juwaiya. I politely asked her to couples skate and there we were holding hands and skating away.

I arranged that we meet on top of the third tier of the steps where all the dancing and vryery took place. Juwaiya and I were smooching on the top tier and besides exchanging saliva, we exchanged home phone numbers, much to Cassiem's dismay.

Boytjie, gaan maak reg jou hare.

Let's just say Juwaiya arrived with lipstick on and I left with lipstick on. If we didn't skate, we would dance the night away on those steps at Fun City. That night I showed Juwaiya my moves, off and on the ice.

The rest of her night belonged to me. We had good clean fun back in them days, and we did not even have to Facebook message or Insta message a girl. We had to go up and introduce ourselves. We did what we had to do. Just ask Cassiem. And when you got to couples skate with someone, it was all worth it.

Our parents knew exactly where we were, although they didn't always know what we were up to.

No harm in a little ice rink fling though, and nothing more.

True story.

Manresa Farm

IN MY LATE TEENS ONE OF OUR favourite camping spots was at Manresa Farm, located just past Atlantis going up the West Coast of Cape Town.

Now this time of the year the whole of Cape Town was there. It was a big farm with a hall, massive swimming pool, braai areas, volleyball court and they even had horseback riding.

We arrive at Manresa and immediately pitched our tents. Fiekie and Fazlin were with and also Aunty Nessa and Boeta Gakkie from Bo-Kaap. We nogals got a top site this time, near the pool area. Faeez and I decide to do our rounds just to go check out who's on camp. I'm speaking under correction, but I think the campsite could host about 400 people.

Walking through the tent site we see a few gangsters from Kensington we know, some familiar faces from the Bo-Kaap, Crawford was in the house, Surrey Estate beauties were spotted, Salt River and Woodstock represented and some of the sturvy kinnes from Walmer Estate even made their way to the camp this year. And then we spotted Twiggy, proudly gay, and his entourage. Twiggy and I were lekka chommies, he was like my sista from another mista. And then we saw about nine tents, representing Ridah and the Jappie clan. This was gonna be a fun camp.

Now let me introduce the Jappie clan. Ridah was this very cool laaitie about the same age as us; a good-looking kid with type 1 hair, straight hare mos.

Yoh, the girls used to smaak him mostly for his hair. Then he had a few uncles who were double our size and all rugby players. They were the Belhar clan. They were big, very intimidating, and also very grof – rough guys.

But they were good-looking, and looked exotic, like Coloureds from Panorama. There were some beautiful girls on this camping trip and Faeez and I couldn't contain ourselves. Then there was Ridah's sister, Ragmah. Yoh, she was mooi, nuh.

Announcements were made over the PA to say what events would take place. There was a waterpolo tournament, volleyball tournament, Miss and Mr Manresa contest. A burning (dance) competition. We were so gonna enter the waterpolo and the volleyball tournaments. Little did they know Faeez and I played club volleyball.

Day 1

The waterpolo tournament is about to kick off. We get our team together and of course I have my orange Speedo on. It made me more aerodynamic in the water. Don't ask about the colour.

Games are going well and we are through to the semis. Oh, our team's name was Stokstyf. Once again, don't ask. We beat the Scripture Union team in the semis and through to the finals we go. And who do we meet in the finals, but the Jappie clan. Now like I said, these were moerse uncles and they only know about tackling. The game is going geroek and the scores are tied at five a side. The one Jappie uncle is all over me. I have the ball, swim to the side and the uncle decides to throw his whole body onto me. Now I'm already fighting the water and now there's this uncle to worry about as well.

Yoh, he gives me a few klappe, soema thru the bek. I manage to sneak the ball past the uncle, pass it to Faeez and he slams the ball into the net. Time is up and Stokstyf takes the trophy. After that game I felt like I was in a wrestling match.

Day 2

Volleyball tournament next and Ridah and two of the Jappie cousins joined up with our Stokstyf team. Myself, Faeez and Ridah all have our mangas – those knee-length shorts – on for this tournament. We won our first game and second game and then through to the semis again. Now remember, Faeez and I played school and club volleyball.

And did we show off that day. Soema setting and spiking like it's going out of fashion. Got into the finals and we killed it, hey. Got the trophy and soema a few vouchers for free entry into the jol in the hall that night. The jol was happening and everybody was festive.

Then all changed. I just see one of the gangsters from Kensington flying out of that jol. The guy lands on his face and Twiggy is all over him. I don't know what he said but he clearly upset Twiggy. And Twiggy says to him 'vanaand kry jy op jou moer. Dink jy my hande is tette?' And Twiggy knocks that skollie almost unconscious. Don't mess with my sister. Pick your battles, my boy.

Day 3

The day of the Mr and Miss Manresa competition arrives. Zoeghdie was also with us. A pretty boy mos, so he had to enter. Ridah was his competition so we knew it was gonna be down to the two of them. Ridah won that contest and was the crowd, or shall I say the girls' favourite. But I wasn't there to watch them. I was waiting for the Miss Manresa contest. The bikinis were on show and the girls were strutting their stuff. Twiggy couldn't enter due to some technicality.

Some of those girls walking on those heels were walking like they were walking on eggshells. It wasn't pretty, hey.

One of the girls was doing her thing and toe ons weer kyk, her whole bikini top came loose and daar flash contestant number six soema alles. The crowd went crazy and I think I screamed the loudest. Guess who won that contest!

I think it was a tactic, but one I didn't mind too much.

The rest of the days it was just lekka braaing and swimming and socialising, meeting all kinds of new people and making new friends. Some of those friends I still have today.

Ridah and I are friends to this day and every now and then we reminisce about those amazing times. I wish my kids could experience some of the things we enjoyed. Good clean fun and lots of laughter with good people and a few gangsters, just to spice things up a bit. But Twiggy had that under control.

True story.

Oaklands High School sports at Athlone Stadium

FOR THOSE OF YOU WHO DIDN'T have school sports, haai shame. You missed out. This for me was a highlight of the school year.

It starts out the night before the sports day and my mom is now busy stitching that yellow ribbon onto my vest. I was mos in Yellow House. We had four houses – Yellow, Green, Blue and Red. I am so excited because I was representing my house in high jump and the 800 m.

Early to bed and 6am I am up and ready to go. Oaklands High 1988 at the Athlone Stadium. I was house captain and as we enter the stadium we organise our houses, and almost immediately everyone breaks into song. Now we had some lekka songs, hey. And we used to go at each other all day long.

And take note that all our songs were in Afrikaans 'cause we were mos grof like that. If the kids had to sing one of these songs today it would have sounded something like this: 'Yusuf, Yusuf you're our man; if you can't do it, no one can. Go Yusuf!'

Lemme run a few songs or one liners by you and see if you remember. 'Julle kan vir ons maar lo-o-o-oer'. 'Hier kom onse WP, daar gaan julle Aaapie'. 'Oes oes daar hol hulle, oes oes daar hol hulle'. 'Dis 'n geel huis ding, hojaa, 'n lekka lekka geel huis ding, en ons kannie worry nie, want ons gaan we-e-e-e-e-en, dis 'n geel huis ding'. 'zeekalaka wella iyaamba, zeekalaka wella iyaamba'. Don't ask me what that meant; I just know it sounded cool when 1 500 kids sang it at the same time and dancing to it.

And there were many other songs. The egg sandwiches are now flowing in the stands, and the Oros is washing it down nicely. Watse Energade and Powerade.

Insauf and Fatima were our cheerleaders and they kept that Yellow House crowd going. Announcement on the PA goes: 'Can the open high jumpers report to the high jump area please.'

My fokken nerves is klaar, but there are girls everywhere so you can't show it. Off I go. There were about eight competitors for the high jump event – two per house. The bar started at 1.5 m and everybody glides over that height. When we got to about 1.7 m there were only four of us left.

I knew Faroeki was my competition and the other two were gonna fall out soon. At 1.8 m it's Faroeki and myself left. Yellow House is cheering 'Yusie, Yusie, Yusie'.

I felt like I was at the Olympics, meanwhile we were only at 1.8 m. I go first. Ready for my run-up and off I go. About 10 steps in, I plant my left foot into the ground and shoot off up into the sky. Jarre, like Clark Kent I fly over that crossbar.

The Yellow House crowd went absolutely befok. I land on the mat, give the crowd a little wave and now I'm thinking 'Faroeki, wie's jou nannas'. Faroeki is up next and I can see he's lekka nervous. He takes his time running up and I'm saying in my head, 'God please let Faroeki fail, fall or gly on his bek'. And boom, my Du'ah was accepted. Faroeki hit the pole. He had two more turns and I made the same Du'ah three times. Consistency mos. Third time and he hits the crossbar again. I am now the official high jump champion of 1988 at Oaklands High. I asked the judges to raise the bar to 1.83 m, want nou wil ek mos afshow. Cleared 1.83 m and my house went crazy. So that is the highest I jumped. Ja ja, it wasn't 2.2 m but it felt good.

Every hour they would read out the points of the different houses and we would go crazy. Arme Green House was always last. Yes, you guessed it, Yellow House was in the lead.

One of my best friends, Faeez, was now at the javelin with his yellow vessie, and he always won that competition hands down. Yoh, he would moer that javelin, hey. Like 20 m further than everybody else. He nogals made the SASSSA team that year. No man, I'm not talking about the pensioner team. I think it was called South African Senior Schools Sports Association (SASSSA). I also came second in the 800 m and darem brought some more points to my house. That blerry Lee would always beat me at 800 m. We were both school cross-country runners, so I knew it was gonna be tough. Du'ahs didn't work when it came to Lee. That thing ran like Forrest Gump.

The day is coming to a close and the teachers' race is the last one. I have never seen so many hamstrings being pulled in one race. Yoh, they were unfit. Soema one or two would fall at the finish line.

All in good spirit though. Yellow House won that year, and it was so fitting because it was my last year of high school. Bragging rights for the rest of the year, and we rubbed it in!

Best feeling ever was when I walked up into the stands and everybody is cheering for you after that high jump victory. Kisses are coming from all over, and Yusie mos loved it.

Faroeki soema didn't speak to me for a few days after that. Haaties.

Those were just some of the great school sports memories, but I could go on and on. Remember, there were still interschools to come, and that was epic. Shame, my 1.83 m didn't go very far at the interschools. It was all in good spirit though and fun was at the order of the day.

True story.

Matric year at Oaklands High – Club Naughty

THIS WAS THE YEAR WHERE A FEW friends and myself decided we were going to participate in just about everything the school had to offer. It was a year never to be forgotten. And so it begins.

Let me introduce you to some of the people who played a major role throughout this year in my life. Faeez (the javelin thrower from my school sports story) had a bit of a crazy streak and was bets for just about everything.

Abduraghmaan (Maan) was very athletic, had good hair and was a little shy. Yusie Dik was just as crazy as me and we were always in trouble with the teachers. They used to call us Yusie Dik and Yusie Din.

Zaid was also athletic and always game for anything. Not Faeez' cousin for nothing.

Nizaam was very athletic and had a great sense of humour. The two of us sang *Lady in Red* in front of the whole class one day, like an Oaklands *Idols* competition.

Although, I think if I had to do a solo, I would have won it. Don't tell Nizaam.

Hiema Bubble had one of those *A-Team* panel vans with a bed in the back. I'm gonna leave that one right there.

Then there were the girls who formed part of our group. Siyaam, Amina, Fatima, Insauf, Hadiyah, Shanaaz, Sumaya, Rashieka, Zulfah. Oh and there was Gakkie, who was at Rylands High but was part of our group.

We decided to start our own social club and called it Club Naughty. We had jackets made similar to our school colours so we could wear it every day at school. Jitte, we were kwaai. We had meetings every Friday and even raised some funds.

Here's just a few incidents that happened around this group. So, one day we are all kitted out in our jackets, getting ready for ten-pin bowling. We all lived in Surrey Estate or Primrose Park. We're all walking to Siyaam's House in Aries Road as our meeting spot.

Now, we're waiting outside her house for the rest of the gang to arrive and just chatting away. As we stand in the street we see Hiema coming up the road in his Ford Escort. About 200 m away I'm thinking let me step onto the pavement out of Hiema's way because he was a bit of a crazy driver.

Everybody but one person follows suit. Now remember I told you Faeez (Eezy) was a bit crazy? Hiema is heading straight for us, picking up speed. Eezy moves to the middle of the road. Opens up his arms like saying to Hiema: 'Jy kan mos lekke kyk of jy vir my kan om stamp?'

Hiema is putting foot down, and Eezy kap vas. Who the hell plays chicken with a car? Hiema steps more on the gas and Eezy mos thinks he's Superman. Next thing we hear is 'bah!' There goes Superman about 10 m up in the sky. Jy wil mos vlieg.

Hiema knocks the shit out of Eezy, who comes crashing

down about 20 m further while we are still trying to figure out what the heck just happened.

And I'm thinking 'fokkit I'm still going to ten-pin bowling'.

Long story short, we ended up in hospital with Superman, who now had a broken leg.

Next episode was at school where we entered the Miss Valentine competition. Yes, it was an all boys Miss Valentine contest. I soema got Insauf's white dress. We basically all wore a dress of one of the girls in our group. Make-up was applied and we are practising our cat-walks backstage.

Now I had a slim figure back then so it was easy for me to get into a dress. Some of the other guys though – let's just say the dresses were just a bietjie tight. Show starts, and we are parading in front of the whole school and all our teachers. The crowd is going crazy and we are just striking all kinds of poses. And of course, Eezy had to take it to another level. Soema some hectic dance moves in his tight dress. Stole the show and was crowned Miss Valentine. I had to settle for first princess. He knew I looked better than him in my dress so he had to perform. But okay, I got over it a few years later and we're still friends.

Next was the Oaklands and Trafalgar High Rag. Ah, this day was special. The principals of the two schools were twins, so every year we used to compete against one another in all kinds of sport. The highlights were the rugby and volleyball.

I was on the volleyball team. Myself, Eezy, Zaid, Nizaam, Maan, Wanie, Dullah, Allan, Emile and Shaun (Lippe). Why Lippe? Because let's just say he had a fuller set of lips than the rest of us. He was a great sportsman and a crazy character. We had an awesome volleyball team.

Yusie Dik was on the rugby team. All the volleyball guys had lekka hair so that's one of the reasons we didn't play rugby. The rugby guys were 'n klomp vuilgatte. But they were all my friends.

We beat Trafs volleyball team every year I was there playing in my powder-blue manga.

Now our girls weren't very sporty, except Tracy (Tasneem) who played volleyball with us. Nog 'n crazy one. Our girls were some of the prettiest at Oaklands. Busy bunch though and loads of fun.

Some of the girls worked in the tuckshop at school; needless to say we didn't pay for that Man's Meal pie and that guava juice. Can't mention any names though, but you know who you are. I hope you girls asked God for forgiveness. I was never gonna take the free pie and juice, but I felt that peer pressure kicking in, so I had to.

Most of the guys were house captains at the school sports and the girls were cheerleaders. Fatima and Insauf were leading that cheerleader pack. They were kwaai nogals and that's why Yellow House won.

Yusie Dik and myself also participated in a play, which was my acting debut. Apparently, I'm up there with Tom Cruise and co – in my mind at least!

Next was the matric ball and I drove my date in my dad's blue VW Beetle. Not the fastest car so it took us a while to get to Muizenberg Civic. Had to leave a bietjie early to get there on time. I've missed out a few more stories because I know this will go on and on.

Overall it was a fantastic and very eventful year with an absolutely great bunch of people I still call my friends today. Memories that will stay with us forever.

True story.

Space Odyssey

LET ME TAKE YOU WAY BACK in time, to a place called the Space Odyssey. Let me introduce you.

I was around 20 years old and this was my hangout every Saturday – and some other days – for about three years. This was a club on Salt River's Main Road and the most happening spot at the time. Best music, best DJ and the most beautiful girls Cape Town had to offer. For my friends and I, this was the main attraction.

Let me explain the build-up to a typical Saturday night at the Space. Now my friends and I all worked at clothing stores in town. After work we would all meet at London Hair Academy where Lyon would prepare our hair. We were about eight friends and we all decided we were going to grow our hair long. Now not all of us could pull off long hair, but we were such kwaai chommies that even if you looked kak, your friends would all say you look befok. Die klomp liegbekke.

Remember the bob hairstyle? Yip, we all had a bob,

or so we thought. So Lyon is now moering our hair with that hairdryer and the hair products are going around left right and centre. That was stop number one. Half the pay cheque in its glory. Sometimes when Lyon wasn't available Zoeghdie's cousin Ganiefah used to give us all a blowjob. With the hairdryer. That was stop number two. Walk across to the Grand Parade and get a lekka atchaar chip roll at Quality Foods, and a Frulati. Dik gevriet en met mooi hare, off we go to my house in District Six. We were mos the first Coloureds to move back there.

Now it's around 4pm, and it's time to sort out who's wearing what. Almal dra almal se klere. That sorted, everyone goes home to take a nap before meeting back at my house at around 10pm. Lekka uitgerus and ready to go for our night at the Space.

Now we used to skud in two Nissan 1400 bakkies, which was mos now not the coolest mode of transport, but fok, our hair was lekka and we were ge-yak, looking good. Cowboy boots and all.

Now let me give you a brief description of my seven chommies.

Zoeghdie: Good looking boy, very naughty and had vuil plak – quite ballsy. He would go up to the hottest girl in the club, and if you look again, they're busy vrying.

Faried: He had the best body (won Mr Le Club mos), and the girls loved him. And he was over his hair.

Sharkie: Good looking, kwaai hair and that Cindy Crawford mole mos. Sweetest guy ever. Girls loved him. And some boys.

Zahir: He was a brat and always had two girlfriends, and they would both sit in front in the bakkie. Don't ask me how he did that. Practising for those seven wives to come, maybe.

Omar: Gone too soon. He was Sharkie's brother. He was just perving. Kak funny and loved by everyone.

Shawaan: Very komieklik – the funny guy – and he had the moves.

Faghmie: He danced till the DJ said at five in the morning, 'ladies and gentlemen, final song.'

Nathier: Now he was bigger than all of us. He was a lifeguard and didn't take shit from anyone. He had our backs, always.

Right, that's my crew.

As you enter the club, there's a little raised platform on your left with a small drinks area. To your right, down three steps, you reach the dance floor. Behind the dance floor was the bar and restaurant. Russell (the love muscle) was in the DJ box doing his thing. He was befuk, nuh.

I was friends with Russell and that meant I had perks. It went like this: before Russell plays the blues songs – slow songs – he would signal me and I would then relay the message to the boys. This meant that now you position yourself right next to the girl that you have had your eye on the whole night. So I'm into position, next to the absolutely gorgeous Lucretia. And I'm thinking 'vanaand is it aan'.

As he plays the slow songs, I jump right in front of Lucretia and asked: 'Would you like to blues, please?'

Yes, I was a gentleman and always said please. And if they said no then my response was: 'I was just joking, I don't really want to blues with you.'

On this night it was a yes. Off into the crowd, Chappies in my mouth, lights off and we are now holding each other and bluesing the night away. Now if a girl didn't like you then after the first song she would say thank you and move on. Not Lucretia. We bluesed soema all six songs, and all I remember was when the lights went back on, I had lipstick all over my face. I swear it was all self-defence, again. She actually became my girlfriend after that night. Lovely girl.

Sometimes you would dance the night away and all of a sudden you hear 'Gadija, your father is waiting for you in the foyer'. Hahaha. Worst thing that could happen to you.

Gadija never came back to that club. Then the jazz numbers come on. Now not all guys could jazz. But in my crew, most of us could jazz. We mos practised at the Galaxy on a Thursday night how to jazz, instead of going to the Gadat. Don't judge us, we were young and lekka loskop. Be that as it may, we had some of the best and most fun times in this club.

It was a great night, I had Lucretias' number and we have about six girls on the back of our bakkies on our way to Golden Dish to end off the night.

Good clean fun was at the order of the day, unlike some of the crap going on today. Space Odyssey was a legendary place where we made friends that are still there today. But if I look back at the pics of us back then, those poor girls didn't also maar have much options. Bless their souls.

True story.

Wedding moments – betaal jou maskawie

A MUSLIM WEDDING IS TRULY an experience you won't forget in a hurry. You're in for a treat and bring a big bag with, because the food, the flower arrangements and soema everything on that table will find its way into that bag. When the wedding is over, you would think there was never food on that table. Die aunties en uncles maak skoon.

This is how it usually went down.

Wynberg Civic Centre is booked. The food is organised. Back then all the cousins were asked to be waiters at the wedding, if you didn't make it as a best man or bridesmaid. The wedding cars are organised. Obviously they have to be kwaai cars. Those few rich uncles that you know lent their cars of course. And so it begins.

On the big day, the groom is off to the mosque on his own, where he meets the bride's father. The Imam – Muslim priest – performs the nikkah, or marriage contract. The groom hands over to the bride's dad an amount of money or gold coin or whatever the bride asked for. That is called the maskawie. Done, they are married.

The groom is now off to finally see his bride, waiting for him at another hall. They exchange rings and take a few pics and are ready for the long day's proceedings. All the uncles who were at the mosque are now having tea and treats at this hall. Not all of them are invited for the lunch, so they must maar eat lekka.

The bride wears her morning wedding gown and as soon as they have exchanged rings and had the pics taken, she goes back home and changes into her next wedding gown.

Now off to Wynberg Civic. The wedding lunch has been organised by the bride's family and the dinner later by the groom's family at Sea Point Civic. Bride and groom walk into the hall with all the little pageboys and flower girls following. Behind them are the four best men and four bridesmaids.

The bride is sporting her draad midowra (headgear) and her second dress for the day. Now you know when you're the cute one in the family, you are always asked to be best man or bridesmaid. Haaties for the rest.

The *Titanic* theme song is playing as they walk in (not a good song for a wedding by the way, seeing the RMS *Titanic* went down). Just saying. The aunties and uncles are now scrutinising the couple and all kinds of whispers are going around that hall. Sometimes not even whispers, soema out loud.

Let me share some of the things I've heard people say as the couple walks in. 'Oe ja, she mos has a child from another man'. 'Jinne, but she's glowing, are you sure she's not pregnant?' 'They mos gonna live in the separate entrance by his parents' 'They broke up twice already,

I wonder if this marriage is gonna last'. 'No, she's from Mitchell's Plain and his parents live in Rondebosch East mos. Sy val met haar gat in die botter'. 'I hope she's gonna keep that figure, come talk to me after the first baby and dan kyk jy hoe lyk daai gat'.

This was just some of the chatter I heard over my years of going to weddings. Ai ja, my people, bless their souls.

Now the couple sit down on the stage for all to admire. There's always that one stoutgat pageboy that has to perform. The one who will do backflips on the stage and just won't sit still for the photos.

Finally, lunch is served.

Here's some of the chatter that goes down. 'Oooh, the breyani was lekka nuh but the potatoes were a bit hard'. 'Oooh nooo, by the time the food got to the table, it was cold'. 'Daar was nie genoeg drinks op die tafel nie'. And, and, and. You could never please everyone, but they vriet themselves into a coma with that breyani. And what was left of that food went into a Tupperware container that was stashed in that moerse big handbag.

Then there was always that one uncle that was put in charge of the mic, doing speeches like he was Trevor Noah. Ai ja, we had to listen to some seriously flou jokes. Sometimes soft music would be playing and sometimes there were a few uncles all sitting at one table who belonged to the same Malay choir that would break out in song.

All family members and friends now had to go up the stage to take pics with the happy couple. After lunch the couple is whisked off to Claremont Gardens for the afternoon photoshoot. When done with the gardens, she goes home and puts on her third dress and off it is to the groom's dinner reception at Sea Point Civic.

The same process repeats itself there and the couple by now just want to go home. I wonder why? When all is done and most people have left, the Hadjies – the older ladies who went on Pilgrimage to Mecca – walk her out of the reception hall. Everybody is crying now while all this is happening. Don't ask me why, please.

And off to the bruidskamer – the bridal bedroom – which everybody is now first inspecting. This room probably took that boy's dad about six months to prepare for this special day. That poor man worked his gat off to get it done on time. But it was always ready to move into.

Six months later the couple will have a lovely baby boy and that aunty who sat at the one table was spot on when she said the bride was glowing. Just kidding!

If we as kids must know what our parents sometimes go through to make this day happen, we would always be grateful to them. Parents sometimes break their backs and their banks just to make sure their kids have this perfect wedding day. How can we not love and respect them for loving, caring and giving us such a great send-off?

Next time you go to a Muslim wedding, don't forget to take the flower arrangements home with you. Just make sure you have enough space in your boot, next to the Tupperware bakke that you filled with the left-over breyani.

True story.